The Thief Hunt

Level 8 – Purple

Helpful Hints for Reading at Home

The graphemes (written letters) and phonemes (units of sound) used throughout this series are aligned with Letters and Sounds. This offers a consistent approach to learning whether reading at home or in the classroom.

HERE IS A LIST OF PHONEMES FOR THIS PHASE OF LEARNING. AN EXAMPLE OF THE PRONUNCIATION CAN BE FOUND IN BRACKETS.

Phase 5			
ay (day)	ou (out)	ie (tie)	ea (eat)
oy (boy)	ir (girl)	ue (blue)	aw (saw)
wh (when)	ph (photo)	ew (new)	oe (toe)
au (Paul)	a_e (make)	e_e (these)	i_e (like)
o_e (home)	u_e (rule)		

Phase 5 Alternative Pronunciations of Graphemes			
a (hat, what)	e (bed, she)	i (fin, find)	o (hot, so, other)
u (but, unit)	c (cat, cent)	g (got, giant)	ow (cow, blow)
ie (tied, field)	ea (eat, bread)	er (farmer, herb)	ch (chin, school, chef)
y (yes, by, very)	ou (out, shoulder, could, you)		

HERE ARE SOME WORDS WHICH YOUR CHILD MAY FIND TRICKY.

Phase 5 Tricky Words			
oh	their	people	Mr
Mrs	looked	called	asked
could			

TOP TIPS FOR HELPING YOUR CHILD TO READ:

- Allow children time to break down unfamiliar words into units of sound and then encourage children to string these sounds together to create the word.

- Encourage your child to point out any focus phonics when they are used.

- Read through the book more than once to grow confidence.

- Ask simple questions about the text to assess understanding.

- Encourage children to use illustrations as prompts.

PHASE 5 /ie/

This book focuses on the grapheme /ie/ and is a purple level 8 book band.

The Thief Hunt

Written by
Robin Twiddy

Illustrated by
Drue Rintoul

Let me tell you a tale of mistrust, of bickering and broken friendships. Let me tell you the tale of the Thief Hunt. It began here, in this hut, with a thing that was missing.

All the grown-ups had left. The kids were getting their bags when Dave noticed something.

"Hey, I had a movie on DVD! It's gone!" Dave said as he spun around to face the others.

"Who did it? Who took my movie?" Dave growled at the other scouts. "It's got zombies in it! I love zombies." Dave pointed a finger at Beth. "Was it you?" he yelled.

"It wasn't me," cried Beth. "Besides, my wellies are gone too."
"Well, someone took it…" Dave began.
"… And my wellies," interrupted Beth. "Don't forget my wellies."
"And her wellies," said Dave. "One of you is the thief!"

Soon, the hut was filled with accusing shouts and pointing fingers. A voice cut through the din.

"The thief took my undies!" said Tim, pulling his waistband out and looking deep into his trousers.

"You don't wear undies," Dave replied.
"Oh, you're right. Never mind," said Tim, releasing is waistband with a ping.
"Well, it wasn't me or Beth," said Dave.
"We have both been robbed."

Dave locked the door. "No one leaves until we find the thief!"

Fred stepped forward. "Who has something missing?" he asked. Fred liked to think of himself as being in charge. "Check all pockets and bags."

Kim was missing her handkerchief; Bill had lost some sweeties and Jazz was missing a cookie, although she did have specks of cookie on her lips. It was clear how big the problem was getting.

A girl with a notebook stepped forward. "It is time for some applied science," she said. Her name was Val and she wanted to be a police officer when she grew up.

Val pulled out a round piece of glass and began to look around.
"Interesting… mmm." All the kids watched her investigate. If Val could find the thief, they could all go home.

Val stood up with an "Ah ha!"
"I found out who the thief is!" she said with a smile. She held up a pen dripping with a strange, green slime. "It must have been an alien!"

"Uh," sniffed Basil, "I don't think it was an alien." He followed this up with a sneeze that added a second pool of slime to the floor. "Ew," said Val as she dropped the pen.

A kid in a hoodie pushed past the crowd.
"I have to go," he said.
"No way!" said Dave, blocking the door.
"No one sets foot on that field out there until we find the thief."

"Tip his bag out!" screamed Dave.
The rest of the scouts gathered around the boy in the hoodie. Snatching hands ripped his bag from his arms and emptied its contents onto the floor.

Puppies fell from the bag and scampered off into the corners of the hut.

"No!" shouted the boy in the hoodie, as he dashed after one of the puppies. "I told you it wasn't me!"

"You can't keep puppies in a backpack," said Val.
"But they like it," replied the boy in the hoodie. One of the puppies went to the toilet in his bag.

Fred insisted that they all emptied their bags. Pens, notebooks, yoyos and all sorts of things spilled onto the floor. But there was no zombie movie, no wellies and no sweeties.

"I can't take this," yelled a girl. Her name was Annie and she was fed up. "Whoever the thief is, just give us back our stuff and we can all go home."
The room was silent. No one moved.

"OK, let's all close our eyes and count to ten," said Annie. "The thief can put all the stolen things back, and no one will ever see who it was."

All the kids closed their eyes and counted to ten. When they opened their eyes, the missing things had not turned up. In fact, more things had vanished!

The floor was clear. All the things from their bags had gone. All except the puppies. The boy in the hoodie was still catching them all.

"You baddies," cried Val, "you're all in on it!" she screamed. Val grabbed Fred by the collar and started to look down his top. "What are you hiding down there?

"It's just my tum," said Fred, with a little hint of sadness in his voice. Val let go and Fred fell to the floor.
Things had gotten tense, and feelings were getting hurt.

The kids were soon bickering again. Fingers were poked in painful places; toes were stepped on and names were being called. Annie's glasses fell to floor. This was not how scouts acted.

In all the noise and mayhem, no one noticed the birdie hop down from the open window. No one noticed the birdie pick up Annie's glasses. And no one noticed the same bird leave out the open window.

Often, when we look for something – such as a missing DVD – what we find instead is something about ourselves. But where did all the things go? Ask a crow!

The Thief Hunt

1. What was the first item to go missing?
   - (a) Glasses
   - (b) A movie
   - (c) Puppies

2. Val wanted to be a police officer when she grew up. What do you want to be when you grow up?

3. Did an alien steal anything? Where did the green slime come from?

4. Who was the thief all along?

5. Have you ever had anything stolen from you? How did you deal with it?

© 2022 **BookLife Publishing Ltd.**
King's Lynn, Norfolk, PE30 4LS, UK

ISBN 978-1-80155-475-6

All rights reserved. Printed in Poland.
A catalogue record for this book is available from the British Library.

The Thief Hunt
Written by Robin Twiddy
Illustrated by Drue Rintoul

An Introduction to BookLife Readers...

Our Readers have been specifically created in line with the London Institute of Education's approach to book banding and are phonetically decodable and ordered to support each phase of the Letters and Sounds document.

Each book has been created to provide the best possible reading and learning experience. Our aim is to share our love of books with children, providing both emerging readers and prolific page-turners with beautiful books that are guaranteed to provoke interest and learning, regardless of ability.

BOOK BAND GRADED using the Institute of Education's approach to levelling.

PHONETICALLY DECODABLE supporting each phase of Letters and Sounds.

EXERCISES AND QUESTIONS to offer reinforcement and to ascertain comprehension.

BEAUTIFULLY ILLUSTRATED to inspire and provoke engagement, providing a variety of styles for the reader to enjoy whilst reading through the series.

AUTHOR INSIGHT:
ROBIN TWIDDY

Robin Twiddy is one of BookLife Publishing's most creative and prolific editorial talents, who imbues all his copy with a sense of adventure and energy. Robin's Cambridge-based first class honours degree in psychosocial studies offers a unique viewpoint on factual information and allows him to relay information in a manner that readers of any age are guaranteed to retain. He also holds a certificate in Teaching in the Lifelong Sector, and a postgraduate certificate in Consumer Psychology.

Robin specialises in conceptual, role-playing narratives which promote interaction with the reader and inspire even the most reluctant of readers to fully engage with his books.

This book focuses on the phoneme /ie/ and is a purple level 8 book band.